The California Mission Story

Fray Junípero Serra, 1713 - 1784.

D1260466

The sweep and grandeur of the West comes to sharp focus in the saga of the California Missions.

The story begins on January 9, 1769, when the ship *San Carlos* sailed from La Paz in Baja California for the port of San Diego. Two other vessels left at a later date, one of them lost at sea. Junípero Serra, the Apostle of California, travelled with the land expedition led by Gaspar de Portolá. Making their way through unexplored desert, the Spanish soldiers carried their water with them in bags and casks. They did not know when they would encounter their next stream.

These men, with cross and sword, gained and dominated the Pacific edge of North America for more than half a century. Their grand adventure was a counter-thrust, by King Carlos III of Spain, to bold Russian incursions, climaxed by the establishment of Fort Ross on the California coast.

The garb of the missionaries included a gray robe, girded with a knotted cord, sandals, and a wide-brimmed hat as a protection against the weather.

The purpose of the missionaries was to Christianize and civilize the Indians, who were taught to pray, to worship, to work, and to follow the Spanish way of life. Under the direction of Spanish overseers, the Indians did most of the construction work on both missions and presidios. The work at each mission comprised farming, ranching, and such trades as carpentry, blacksmithing, weaving, tailoring, leather products, etc. Conversion was voluntary. But once the Indians became Christians, they were required by Spanish law to reside at the missions. Various causes led to some measure of fugitivism: the natural love of the Indians for the forest, fear of white men's diseases to which the natives easily succumbed, regular hours of work to which they were unaccustomed, and punishment for delinquency. The soldiers were for the protection of the missionaries and the missionized Indians.

Called *soldados a_____ ts"*) to distinguish them from the regular Spanish army, the presidial troops were tough, obedient, resolute and active. They were among the best horsemen in the world. Their defensive equipment included the *cuera,* a jerkin made of six or seven thicknesses of dressed deerskin, impervious to Indian arrows except at very short range, and an *adarga,* a shield made of two thicknesses of raw bull's hide, worn on the left arm.

For offensive weapons they carried a lance, managed from horseback with great dexterity, a broad sword, and a short musket in a leather case. This equipment was so much more effective than Indian bows and arrows. Three soldiers were a match for fifty Indians. A squad of six soldiers formed the usual military guard at each mission.

In 1810 Mexico began her revolution against Spain. Until 1821, when she gained her independence, the supply ships ceased their voyages from San Blas, and Spanish California was on its own. Supplied by the missions, the presidial forces were able to maintain their posts.

Before 1821 a few land grants were made by Spain. After that date many were made by Mexico. The California rancheros flourished.

In 1833 the missions were secularized. Mission lands and herds fell to the rancheros. In 1848 came the Yankees and the end of Hispanic California.

Pehaps the vignettes of 21 missions on these pages will be windows through which to glimpse Serra's ambient dream.

For the mellow mission stone and tile — in just the right late afternoon light — seem to glow with the radiance of a great saint's vision.

This is the essence of the California mission story.

A statue of Padre Junípero Serra, founder of the California missions, stands pensively before the first mission, San Diego de Alcala.

San Diego de Alcalá

Beautiful inner court and garden. The mission was practically destroyed, but various restorations have brought it to excellent condition.

5 Miles East of Highway 5 in Mission Valley, Off State Highway 8.

The California Missions almost never happened!

When San Diego de Alcala, the first mission, was planned in 1769, the Spanish king's hopes for a string of ecclesiastical-military establishments in California hung by a thread.

Everything that could go wrong, did go wrong.

First of all, two expeditions had left Baja California by land and two by sea.

The two ships arrived at San Diego first. When the land expeditions came on the scene, they found that scurvy had stricken the crews of both ships. 38 sailors had died. The *San Antonio*, with a skeleton crew of 8 men, was sent back to San Blas to get fresh supplies for the expedition and new crews for the two ships. The Rivera land expedition of 40 men was also sent back to Baja California for supplies.

Local Indians, the Yumas, were more aggressive, turbulent, and warlike than their relatively peaceful neighbors to the north. Trouble from them could be expected. And it came.

The Spaniards, apparently weak and defenseless, became a target. The Indians planned secretly, assembled and then attacked with a great volley of arrows. Little damage

Massive wood door, round arch are typical of the missions' Mediterranean style.

was done to the leather-armored musketeers, and the braves didn't flinch as the Spaniards fired back . . . until they saw a number of their companions lying dead. Then they realized that their weapons would never be a match for Spanish guns.

Six months later, Governor Portolá, returning from Monterey, found his people in crucial condition. Nineteen more had died. A few rickety buildings housed the remainder. Their supply ship was long overdue.

Portolá decided that, unless it arrived by March 19, 1769 (the feast of St. Joseph), he would cancel the expedition and order a return to Mexico.

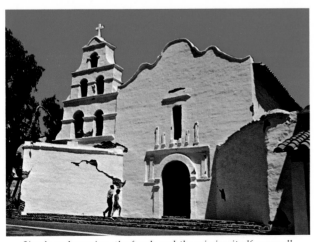

Simple and massive, the facade and the mission itself, were all but destroyed by a violent Indian attack in 1775.

Three-tiered campanario lends grace note to solid structure. Bell at lower right, 1200 lb. Mater Dolorosa, was cast from five bells sent by viceroy in 1796.

Serra prayed almost continuously for the swift return of the San Antonio. On the evening of March 19 sails were sighted, then they disappeared below the horizon again.

The governor decided to hold out a little longer — and in a few days the San Antonio laden with supplies, dropped anchor in the harbor.

The mission system was back in business!

Within a month, Portolá headed north by land, Serra by sea — destination Monterey! Objective — founding of the second Mission.

CHRONOLOGY

1769 — July 16 — Founded by Padre Junípero Serra. First mission. Named for Didacus of Alcala.	1780 — Rebuilt.
	1801 — Damaged by earthquake.
	1833 — Secularized. (Missions disbanded by Mexican decree.)
1774 — Moved from Presidio Hill above Old Town to present site.	1845 — Sold.
	1862 — Returned to church.
1775 — Burned in Indian attack.	1931 — Rebuilt.

San Carlos Borromeo de Carmelo

Reredos in the main church. Brilliant colors match those of original work. Gothic arch at top of picture is only one in mission chain.

Just South of City of Carmel Near State Highway 1.

Warm and mellow as fine old brandy, Carmel mission casts a mystic spell on visitors. Perhaps it's the interplay of contrasts and harmonies . . . green mountains and blue sea, rough sandstone church with lush garden, darting swallows and sonorous, full-skirted bells.

In preparation for founding the second Mission, the ship San Antonio sailed from San Diego on April 16, 1770 with Father Serra — and a cargo of supplies for the new mission to be founded on the shores of Monterey Bay.

They were to meet a land party which left San Diego a few days later, captained by Portolá with his Lieutenant Fages, twelve Catalonian volunteer soldiers and seven *sol-datos de cuera,* Padre Crespi, two muleteers and a few Indian laborers.

They reached Monterey a week before the San Antonio and found the cross planted there by Portolá on his earlier expedition. The cross was now surrounded with arrows, sticks, feathers, fish, meat and clams, deposited by the natives as offerings to the Spaniards' fetish.

Later when the Indians had learned to communicate with them, they told strange tales of the cross, saying it had been mysteriously illuminated at night and at times, grew tall enough to reach the heavens.

On June 3, 1770, on the beach at Monterey, assembled under an *enramada* (shelter of branches), a new cross was readied, water was blessed and Padre Junípero put on his alb (long white linen robe with tapered sleeves) and stole (embroidered scarf). Everyone knelt and chanted the *"Veni, Creator Spiritus."* Then the cross was erected and blessed.

Serra sprinkled the beach and the fields with holy water, "putting to rout all infernal foes."

Gold and red of Spain mingle with primitive Indian pigments and designs in the small chapel of the Blessed Sacrament.

Carmel mission and court yard. Note Moorish fountain, asymmetric bell towers, star window, red tile roofs and opulent garden.

Strength of masonry shows in this unplastered church side wall and bell tower.

In this manner was founded San Carlos Borromeo de Monterey (soon to be San Carlos Borromeo del Carmelo). A few huts comprising both mission and presidio, were promptly built.

Padre-Presidente Serra, with the Coast from San Diego to Sonoma as his fiefdom, chose Carmel for home. As the old hymn goes . . . "in all things great and small" . . . the man's judgment was superb.

He found the ideal site "2 gunshots (2600 ft.) from the sea," just south of the present town of Carmel. It took about six months to build a chapel, dwelling, storehouse, and kitchen, surrounded by a stockade.

The existing structure is seventh in a series stretching back to 1771 when the first log shelter was built. Monterey was a poor choice for a mission. The soil was not adequately fertile. The water supply was insufficient for crops. It was the policy of the missionaries to found missions in areas where the natives lived in greater numbers. And it was advisable to keep the Indians at a distance from the presidio.

When it came time to build the final church, Lasuén, Serra's successor, did the planning. In 1791, he ordered stone quarried and imported a master mason, Manuel Ruiz, to design the building.

Ruiz built with a feeling for beauty — demonstrated by charming bell towers of uneven size, one with a Moorish dome, the stone catenary arches, a vaulted ceiling, the unique star window over the front doorway.

Sculptor Jo Mora created the sarcophagus with recumbent statue representing Serra in death. Three kneeling monks are Padre Crespi at the head, with Padres Lasuén and Lopez at the foot of the stone coffin.

Junípero Serra's spartan room. The great man took poverty vows seriously.

Some say the star was originally intended to have been placed on its side as a rectangle instead of balanced, as it is, on one point. A poet wrote that it seems to "have been blown out of shape in some wintry wind, and all its lines hardened again in the sunshine of the long, long summer."

Once established at Carmel, Serra spent most of his traveling time to the various missions strung out 650 miles on Camino Real from San Diego to San Francisco. The short (5'2") genius from Mallorca, took vows of poverty seriously. He lived in a tiny cell 100 yards from the church.

This *Presidente* of the chain of missions, one of the great men of the Americas, had as household furniture a board cot, a blanket, one table, one chair, a chest, a candlestick, a gourd . . . nothing else. He died in 1784.

Silver altar service used by Fray Junípero Serra.

Padres' Library – The first library in California.

Padre's kitchen with beehive oven and wrought iron tools.

Mediterranean domes and arches. The mission looks as though it had been lifted up and transplanted whole from southern Spain.

Ancient cemetery said to contain the bones of 3,000 Indians.

Serra was buried in the existing (sixth) structure of adobe. When the new stone church was finished, it encased the small adobe church. Serra's bones are there today.

Near the end of his life, 71, and suffering from a tubercular infection, Serra spoke to his assistant, Padre Lasuén — soon to be Presidente in his place — about new construction.

"When the stone church is built," he said, "you may place me where you will."

CHRONOLOGY

1770 — June 3. Founded by Serra at Presidio, Monterey. Second mission. Moved to Carmel following year. Named for St. Charles Borromeo, Cardinal, 16th century.

1791 — Present church begun under Presidente-Padre Fermín Francisco de Lasuén.

1797 — Dedicated.

1770 - 1803 — Mission chain headquarters.

1834 — Secularized.

1859 — Returned to Catholic Church.

1884, 1924, 1936 — Restorations.

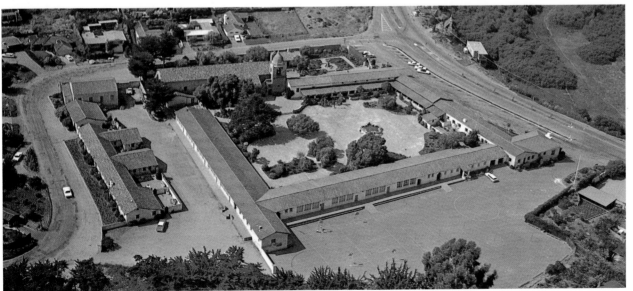

Aerial view shows restored quadrangle with church and auxiliary buildings.

Rebuilt and restored, San Antonio de Padua – in unchanged natural surroundings – gives visitors an insight into what missions were like in their prime.

San Antonio de Padua

A simple statue of St. Anthony in a charming niche.

Burned brick companario opens to barrel-vaulted vestibule.

Off U.S. Highway 101, 27 Miles Northwest of Bradley, 23 Miles Southwest of King City.

Following San Diego and Carmel, San Antonio was the third mission, created by Serra just after he had moved the second mission from Monterey to Carmel. He left soldiers and Indians erecting stockades there, and set off for San Antonio.

He and his party journeyed to the Santa Lucia Mountains, to a place commended by Portolá after his trip two years earlier. They reached a pleasant basin dotted with oaks, and pitched camp on the banks of a stream Serra christened Rio de San Antonio.

The great priest's enthusiasm bubbled over.

When the mules were unloaded, he hung a bell on a tree, started ringing it and calling, "Oh ye gentiles! Come, come to the holy church!" His associates reminded him that there was no church, and no Indians in sight.

Serra explained that he just wanted to "give vent to my heart which desires that this bell might be heard all over the world!"

A bit later, an old Indian woman came to the encampment. She asked to be baptized — thereby astonishing the padres. They hadn't been there long enough for her to know what baptism was, much less develop a desire to participate.

She said her father had told her a story about a man wearing robes who had appeared to him on four occasions and told him of Christianity. The story was related to a well-known Southwest legend. There, in 1620, early mis-

sionaries were surprised to find Indians who apparently were well-informed about the Catholic Church.

The padres checked this and learned of a nun in Spain who said she and others had made many visits, through supernatural teleportation, to the Indians. Though she never left Spain, she backed up her bizarre story with accurate details about Southwest locations and occurrences.

San Antonio got off to a good start. Serra stayed for two weeks, then left the mission in charge of a pair of efficient padres, one of whom was Buenaventura Sitjar.

Main altar with four original statues. Statues were saved by Indians and stored during years when the mission was deserted.

CHRONOLOGY

1771 — July 14 — Founded by Serra. Third mission. Named for St. Anthony.	1813 — Present building completed.
	1834 — Secularized.
1780 — Moved to present site.	1845 — Offered for sale. No takers.
1782 — Adobe church completed.	1882 — Abandoned.
	1907 - 1949 — Restored.

San Gabriel Arcángel

Six thousand Indians are buried here in this, the oldest (1778) cemetery in Los Angeles County.

Companario, unique Spanish wall with holes for bells.

Padre Antonio Cruzado, who built the church, was born at Alcarazegos in Cordoba. The capped buttresses, narrow windows and arched shell decorations of the Cathedral of Cordoba made an indelible impression, and he created them at San Gabriel. After an auspicious beginning, San Gabriel had a cycle of bad relations with Indians. A Spanish rifleman raped the young wife of a local chieftain. The vengeful Indians attacked, determined to kill the culprit. The Indians had courage, bows and arrows. The Spaniards had courage plus powerful muskets and good leather armor. The attack was repulsed, the chief slain on the spot. Eventually, the troubles with Indians diminished, and San Gabriel attained real prosperity.

In the City of San Gabriel on Mission Drive, Ten Miles East of Downtown Los Angeles.

Like Santa Barbara, Mission San Gabriel fascinates the architectural aficionado. The facade is a *side wall* and the main entrance is on the side! Its design is a direct steal from the Cathedral of Cordoba (formerly a Moorish mosque)!

CHRONOLOGY

1771 — September 8 — Founded by Padres Pedro Cambron and Angel Somera. Named for Archangel Gabriel.	1812 — Damaged by earthquake.
	1828 — Repaired.
	1834 — Secularized. Property traded to settle a debt.
1775 — Mission moved to present site.	1859 — Returned to church.
1790 — Present church begun.	1987 — Damaged by earthquake.
1805 — Completed.	

Architecturally intriguing San Gabriel has entry on the side.

San Luis Obispo de Tolosa

High altar is dominated by mission's patron – Saint Louis, 12th Century Bishop of Toulouse.

Corner Monterey and Chorro Streets in Downtown San Luis Obispo.

Don Gaspar de Portolá's expedition, half-starved, was returning to San Diego in 1769, after an unsuccessful search for Monterey harbor. Food was *primero uno* on the agenda as they entered a valley of tule reeds. The ground was dug up . . . and they surmised that grizzly bears had been looking for succulent tule roots.

The presence of game seemed like manna from heaven to the Spaniards, but they discovered that *ursus horribilis* — eight feet tall and 1200 pounds — was hard to handle. By the time they killed a couple of bears, the giant animals had maimed two mules and almost got their riders.

The bear meat feast stayed in the hunters' memories — they named the valley *La Cañada de los Osos*. In 1772, the missions at Carmel and San Antonio ran out of food. A new expedition was organized and shot, salted, and jerked 9,000 pounds of bear meat, plus twenty-five mule loads of edible seeds gained by trading meat to the Indians.

Meanwhile, back at San Luis Obispo de Tolosa, local Indians were friendly but southern tribes were aggressive and hostile. They carried their animosity *right through the roof!* Reed roofs were usually dry as tinder — a few on-target flaming arrows could burn down a whole mission. Presently the padres thought of the fireproof red tiles of Spain. They began to manufacture them then and there. Clay was worked in pits, using horses and burros to knead it to pliability. When ready, clay squares were applied to curved wood forms. After edges were trimmed, tiles dried in the sun and baked in a kiln. Once the tile roofs were in place, fire raids were no longer a problem, interiors consistently dry, and adobe walls shielded from melting rains.

Pieta statuette, pleasing highlight of interior art.

Wishing well in the patio.

CHRONOLOGY

1772 — September 1 — Founded by Padre Serra. Named for St. Louis, Bishop of Toulouse.	1820 — Vestibule added.
	1868 — Modernized with wood siding.
1794 — Present building constructed.	1934 — Restored to original form.

Unusual combination of belfry with vestibule lends interest to severe facade.

Relatively unchanged since completion in 1791, the pretty church has original bells, hanging from rawhide thongs and still rung on holy days.

San Francisco de Asís

San Francisco, Dolores Street Between 16th and 17th Streets.

Inhabitants of today's West, accustomed to up-to-date maps and signs, may have difficulty appreciating the locational mysteries of California in the 1700's. Coastal fogs, the vast continental sweep, hidden harbors (of which San Francisco Bay with its narrow entrance was a prime example), all contributed to the travail of early explorers.

Reredos is a good specimen of Mexican style church art, characterized by rococo gilt.

Five thousand Indians lie in graveyard.

Much time was spent searching for Monterey Bay, which was found the second time around. This was not the case with San Francisco Bay, which was discovered by accident.

When San Francisco Bay was finally explored and charted, it was said that "it could hold all the armadas of Spain." The viceroy ordered two missions and a presidio established there.

Next, Lieutenant Colonel Juan Bautista de Anza, — one of the greatest trail bosses of all time — brought a large party of settlers from San Diego to Monterey. He led 240 people with 1,000 head of cattle over mountains, through deserts and up California's hot valleys with the loss of only one person — a woman who died in childbirth. On arrival in Monterey the party actually consisted of *244* people (several healthy babies were born in route).

Anza continued to San Francisco with a smaller group and picked out a spot for the presidio and one for the mission, the latter on the bend of a little river. This he named *Arroyo de los Dolores* because it was the feast day of "Our Lady of Sorrows." The name became associated with the Mission itself, now generally known as Dolores.

CHRONOLOGY	
1776 — June 26 — Founded by Padre Francisco Palou. Sixth mission. Named for St. Francis of Assisi, founder of Francisco order.	1791 — Dedicated.
	1834 — Secularized.
	1845 — Mission lands sold.
	1857 — Property returned by presidential proclamation.
1782 — Present building begun.	

San Juan Capistrano

In San Juan Capistrano on Interstate Highway 5.

Success . . . tragedy . . . now — the most beautiful ruins in California.

Capistrano had everything going for it from the beginning. In a lovely valley with pleasant climate, and the ground gave an abundance — grains, vegetables, fruit . . . fat cattle grazing on the hills.

Construction proceeded smoothly. Soon there were storehouses, shops, barracks — built around a quadrangle so big that it could hold all the mission Indians and their belongings — a welcome feature in case of Indian raids!

Capistrano prospered and outgrew the original adobe church. In 1796, work on a big stone structure was begun under direction of a Mexican master mason. After nine years of work, he and a crew of Indian laborers finished the cathedral-like church.

It was an imposing edifice. The design was cruciform — one hundred and eight feet long by forty wide. A vaulted ceiling surmounted seven domes. At the entrance was a 120-foot high belltower, visible for ten miles.

The church served well for six years.

At the end of an early morning service in December, 1812, as two Indian boys in the belfry rang for the next Mass . . . there was a deep rumble, a cacaphonic jangle of bells . . . and the roar of a major earthquake. The walls swayed and broke, dumping the concrete ceiling on helpless worshippers.

Only a few who heeded the frantically beckoning padre and rushed to the sanctuary, were saved. Forty bodies

Three-hundred-year-old baroque reredos was imported from Barcelona in the early 19th century.

A white dove finds a home in the adobe wall.

Moorish style fountain in the inner patio is a graceful feature of Capistrano.

Bougainvillea lends a luxurious counterpoint to sturdy arches of the corridor.

These are the most graceful ruins in the mission system. Only the sanctuary remains intact.

Masonry and bells are original.

were dug from the rubble. The boys in the tower were killed, too. But the sanctuary was almost intact . . . fine wooden statues and most furniture unharmed.

The clock-like regularity of the swallows' migration to San Juan Capistrano is celebrated in song and story. Cliff swallows *(petrochelidon pyrrhonota)* swoop down from the sky early in the morning of St. Joseph's day every Spring and begin building gourd-like mud and saliva nests to shelter the new brood. A few come earlier, a few later, but most actually arrive on the saint's day!

The graceful, restless, birds nest under the eaves (at Carmel as well as Capistrano) and contribute in many ways to the missions' mellow atmosphere.

CHRONOLOGY

1775 — October 30. Originally established by Padre Lasuén. Abandoned because of troubles with Indians.

1776 — November 1. Founded by Padre Junípero Serra. Named for St. John of Capistrano, Italy, theologian and inquistor of the Fourteenth Century.

1796 — Stone church begun.

1812 — Destroyed by earthquake.

1833 — Secularized.

1845 — Sold.

1865 — Returned to Church.

Capistrano's mellow beauty is unique.

Present church facade interprets in bas-relief, crude paintings which decorated the original rugged structure.

Santa Clara de Asís

Interior of Santa Clara is not typical of original missions' combination of Spanish baroque and simple Indian designs.

In Santa Clara, on the Alameda.

San Francisco, its harbor enhanced by an easily guarded narrow entry, was an obviously desirable northern bastion for the chain.

So the governor decided to establish two missions and to protect this outpost with a presidio. After Dolores was established, he sent Lieutenant Moraga and Padre Thomas de la Peña, together with a squad of soldiers and their families, to found a new mission — a day's journey south from Dolores.

They headed for the Guadalupe River and, a week later, discovered a good site on the river's banks, forty miles southeast of San Francisco, where they planted a cross on a slight rise, built an arbor for worship and called it Santa Clara de Asis.

There were serious tensions between the people of Mission Santa Clara and those in nearby Pueblo San Jose; problems of ownership, settlers' cattle mingling with mission herds, and disputes over water rights.

Typically, Catalá decided to do something about it. He developed an idea for alleviating tension. With the aid of his soldiers, he rounded up and organized two hundred Indians to link the communities by building a four mile *alameda* between the mission and San Jose. They completed a road with a divider of black willow trees in the center and another row on each side. On Sundays, gaily attired churchgoers, the ladies in silk and satin, all mounted on their handsomest horses, trotted to and from the mission and the town.

The present church facade, ornamented with intaglio designs, is a direct descendent of the original, on which the same ornaments and statuary were painted flat in trompe d'oueil. The big wooden cross erected by Moraga and de la Peña still stands, now sheathed in protective redwood.

CHRONOLOGY

1777 — January 12. Founded by Padre Junípero Serra. Eighth Mission. Named for St. Clare of Assisi, founder of the order "Poor Clares."	1784 — Third church built.
	1819 — Fourth church built.
	1825 — Present church built.
	1836 — Secularization.
1777 — First log church built.	1851 — Transferred from Franciscans to Jesuits.
1779 — Second log church built, near Guadalupe River.	1886 — Remodeled.
	1926 — Burned.
	1929 — Replaced.

San Buenaventura

Heart of Downtown Ventura at 211 East Main Street.

A distinguished cavalcade set out from San Gabriel in March, 1782, to found San Buenaventura. Padre Junípero Serra was the leader. Included were soldiers with their families, priests, provincial officials, muleteers, and pack animals loaded with food, tools and fertilizer. Governor Neve, with ten Monterey cavalrymen, brought up the rear. They headed for a Chumash village (of about 500 inhabitants) known as La Asuncion de Nuestra Senora. On arrival, Serra gave an eloquent sermon and said Mass. Then

they began building a chapel, dwellings and a stockade. Local Chumash were friendly and helpful, and there was plenty to help. The Santa Barbara channel area had twenty-one villages with an Indian population of 10,000.

In 1818, when the pirate, Bouchard, was terrorizing the California coast, his ship was sighted near San Buenaventura. Jose Senan, the priest in charge, hastily gathered mission treasures . . . sacred vessels, vestments, statues, paintings and silver. He buried some things, hid others in a nearby cave. Then, with his followers, he collected baskets of food and camped in the hills for a month, until the danger passed.

The mission prospered. Pleasant climate, good soil and a well-designed irrigation system helped Buenaventura become a center for growing apples, pears, peaches, pomegranates, grapes, olives, and figs. Grain flourished.

Wall around side door has ornamentation the Indians interpreted symbolically. To them it was a chart of the area, with curved lines above the door as the two rivers straddling the mission (indicated by cross). Hills behind church were represented by top line.

CHRONOLOGY

1782 — March 31. Founded by Serra. Ninth mission. Named for St. Bonaventure.	**1842** — Became parish church.
	1845 — Rented by Governor Pio Pico.
1812 — First church destroyed by earthquake.	**1846** — Sold.
	1862 — Returned to church.
1816 — Rebuilt.	**1957** — Restored.
1836 — Secularized.	

Pleasant facade, cream with red trim, has changed little since reconstruction after 1812 earthquake.

Santa Bárbara

The Greco-Roman facade is sharply etched in this early picture of the church. Among the handsomest missions, Santa Barbara is second only to Carmel in popularity. It is unique in many respects, including the fact that, since its founding in 1786, it has been in uninterrupted use.

In the City of Santa Barbara at End of Laguna Street.

Mission Santa Barbara is architectually unique, its beauty deriving from an eclectic design with roots in ancient history.

The towers and general plans resemble those of other missions, but the facade and interior details are unique. Doric columns below a triangular pediment with a reverse swastika fascia . . . classic Greco-Roman . . . designed for a Roman temple *by a man who had been dead for 1800 years before the mission was built!*

Here's how it happened:

In 27 B.C., a Roman architect named Vitruvius Polion authored a work, "The Six Books of Architecture," which was published and republished in Europe through the centuries. A Spanish translation eventually turned up in the mission library.

When the new church was planned, the man in charge was Padre Antonio Ripoll. He admired Polion's work, and lifted every detail of the facade from the "Six Books."

Padre-President Junípero Serra long dreamed of establishing three missions opposite Santa Barbara Channel, with a presidio to protect them to close the gap between San Luis Obispo and San Gabriel.

When Governor Neve started the presidio at Santa Barbara, Serra thought he would soon be building the mission. What he didn't know was that Neve felt that the missions had too much power, and was opposed to further expansion. He persuaded the viceroy in Mexico City to withhold funds for the mission until completion of the presidio.

Main altar and reredos. In the center is a wooden statue of Saint Barbara. Sanctuary light in foreground has burned continuously since 1786.

Majestic and serene, the "Queen of the Missions" stands in a natural amphitheatre formed by the coastline and the Santa Inez Mountains.

So Serra was frustrated — temporarily. It was Padre Lasuén, his successor as Presidente, who actually founded Santa Barbara. But the little genius had the pleasure of knowing, just a month before his death, that the new Governor, Pedro Fages, had given permission to build the mission.

Lasuén chose a site with ample water and a view of the oak-dotted valley, the sea and the channel islands.

The governor attended the dedication in 1786 and the first work was begun the next Spring. Crude buildings were topped with beams, topped by reeds, which were covered with mud and thatch.

Crevices between the logs were filled by mud and stones. Floors were bare earth and the roofs were made of pressed earth and sacate grass.

Since the presidio was built first, the priests lived there until the mission was complete, construction having begun after the spring rains of 1787. The new residence for missionaries was forty-four feet by thirteen feet, nine inches; and the dimensions of the church were thirty-eight feet by six feet by thirteen feet, nine inches. In 1789 a new, adobe church was built and fireproof tile roofing installed for the first time.

Under the direction of Padre Estevan Tapis a new, bigger adobe church — one hundred and twenty-three feet by twenty-five feet, with six side chapels, was completed in 1794, but was severely damaged in the 1812 earthquake. A quadrangle was finished in 1795 and a second adjoining quadrangle begun in 1812. There was a dormitory, kitchen, storeroom and granary, tannery, pottery and warehouse,

Massive cross, on mound of river-rounded stones, in front of the old mission, commemorates Santa Barbara's founding in 1786.

Part of the splendid water system still operating. Mission Dam in Santa Barbara Botanical Garden.

plus two hundred and fifty Indian huts, plastered and whitewashed, with doors and movable windows.

The big Moorish fountain was created in 1808. Its overflow ran into a stone laundry basin where Indian women soaped garments, beat them clean with paddles and rinsed them in clear water. The completed water system was so good that parts of it are still used by the City of Santa Barbara.

Despite the earthquake, the church remained in operation until completion in 1820 of the new stone (present) church, with its facade of Roman arches.

This church, planned and built by Padres Ripoll and Francisco Suñer, *is in use today*, with the same stone facing, contours and ornamentation as the original. It is one hundred and sixty one by twenty-seven by forty-two feet high with towers eighty-seven feet high. One tower was built in 1820, and the second was finished in 1833. The mission living quarters were one-story with flat tile roofs (azotea), and the tile floor of the *corredor* is still to be seen.

Mission Santa Barbara was damaged in a 1925 quake and rebuilt with steel reinforced concrete. The interior has changed little since 1820. The old canvas reredos, statues and paintings are there, and much of the decoration.

Painting of the crucifixion was brought from Mexico in 1800. Exquisite alabaster Pieta statuette was sculpted in Spain in approximately 1250.

St. Francis, founder of the Franciscan order, is depicted in this bronze statue in a hooded cassock with cord belt – a costume derived from Thirteenth Century Italian shepherds. He is associated with love of nature, animals, and peace among men.

Life at Santa Barbara was a busy one for the two friars in charge. They planned buildings, managed farms, supervised livestock raising, kept meticulous records gave religious instruction, learned the local Indian language and administered sacraments.

Typically, there was a division of labor between the two priests according to their personalities. The more idealistic, spirtually dedicated man would concern himself primarily with the church, its ceremony, liturgy, music and the general cause of the Catholic religion on this frontier.

Father Narciso Durán at Santa Barbara was noted for success in music, and produced a Christmas play each year. He trained a band of native musicians and wrote several masses that are still sung in the mission church at this time.

The worldly, practical partner would work on basic problems of food, shelter, clothing and general welfare of the Indian neophytes, the priests and their acolytes and the fifty or more leather-jacketed cavalrymen of the presidio guard. He was aided by a civilian majordomo who acted as overseer of the Indian laborers.

The priests hired civilian craftsmen to teach the Indians skills essential to accomplishing the general development and prosperity of the missions. Needed trades were many. Success was accomplished in teaching farming, cattle and sheep raising, tanning and leather work, including manufacture of saddles and harnesses, sandals and leather strips for lashing timbers together in construction, as well as making soap and candles, and blacksmithing.

In the building trades, Indians became quite adept — with a rough, unsophisticated style — at adobe manufacturing, stone-cutting, masonry, and tile-making.

Santa Barbara Indians belonged to the same tribe and spoke the same Chumash language as those near Buenaventura Mission, but with varied dialects. Near Santa Barbara, when the Spaniards first arrived, male natives went naked, but the women wore rabbit and deer skins.

The coast here was thickly settled, with 10,000 natives concentrated between San Buenaventura and Point Concepción. The Indians slept on rush beds in conical reed huts of various sizes with straw — thatched roofs — small for families — big for meeting places — in large, well laid-out villages.

At the present location of the city of Santa Barbara, there was a village called Yanonalit, with a population of about 500, ruled by a chief of the same name.

The dead were buried in big cemeteries, with painted poles with the hair of the deceased fastened at the top, indicating graves of the men. Those of the women adorned with *cora* — grass baskets. Large whale bones used as markers were another feature of these graveyards.

Rich vestments were sent from Mexico in 1800. The sheet music in photo was written by padres: red, black and yellow notes helped Indian choirs follow multi-part songs.

Missionary's hat and staff — The broad-brimmed hat afforded sun and rain protection. Staff, surmounted by cross (also note hook), was used for a variety of purposes.

The Pacific was a major food source for the Chumash in this area — they were fishermen, clever in maneuvering in coastal waters. Their canoes, twenty-four feet long, made of pine boards tied by cord, were coated with asphalt, and capable of carrying a crew of ten. They frequently journeyed to and from the nearby Channel Islands.

They were fond of paint and bright plumage for dancing and war and, while they fought each other on a village-to-village basis, they were friendly and hospitable towards the Spaniards.

A nefarious Argentine rebel and pirate, Hippolyte Bouchard, was harrying California in 1818, plundering towns and spreading revolt. His reputation, and that of his buccaneers, for arson and banditry was so extravagant that the mere sight of his ship was enough to cause instant evacuations of coastal communities.

But not at Santa Barbara.

Bouchard and his men landed at Refugio Beach, above Santa Barbara, and in a skirmish with the Spanish lost several prisoners. Then he sailed on to the town and anchored. Promising not to engage in further hostilities, he sent a man ashore under a flag of truce, recovered his prisoners, and sailed away.

CHRONOLOGY

1786 — December 4. Founded by Padre Lasuén; tenth mission. Named for Saint Barbara.	1831 — Second tower added.
	1832 — Collapsed.
1794 — Third church built.	1833 — Rebuilt.
1812 — Destroyed by earthquake.	1834 — Secularized.
	1846 — Sold.
1815 — Present church begun.	1865 — Returned to Church.
1820 — Completed with one tower.	Only mission never abandoned, and in continuous use.

Low-growing agave and weeping willow frame the serene Graeco-Roman facade of the mission.

Beautifully restored, Purísima commands a fine prospect of surrounding farmlands.

La Purísima Concepción

19 Miles West of Buellton.

From 1812 onward no supplies were brought from San Blas for the presidios, which came to depend entirely on the missions for their support — food, clothing, leather goods, blankets, lance heads, etc. This already heavy burden was made more onerous still by the arrival of 100 more troops from Mexico after the attack by the pirate Bouchard. Tension grew. Abuse by some of the soldiers inflamed it. The unreasonable flogging of an Indian by a member of the military guard at Mission Santa Ines was a spark that set off an explosion of Indian violence in 1824. Revolt broke out at the mission.

When the news reached La Purisima, the Indians went wild. With rebels from Ines, they seized the church and fortified the grounds. They built stockades, knocked loopholes in the walls, and mounted two cannon. Thus fortified they held off the attacking soldiers for four weeks.

When the governor heard of the crisis, he sent a troop of cavalry, with artillery, from Monterey. The soldiers pounded away at the adobe walls with their cannon. The Indians responded in kind, but most of their shots went wild. Spanish horsemen circled in back and cut off retreat.

In three hours it was over. Padre Rodriguez, who had stayed inside with the Indians in an effort to protect the soldiers' families, came out with a white surrender flag. There were sixteen Indians killed and many wounded . . . one soldier died and three were wounded. Retribution was swift. Seven Indian leaders were executed and twelve sentenced to jail terms.

Unusual main altar before reredos of trompe d'oueil marble background and dramatic "sunburst" niches.

Beautifully carved confessional is an interior highlight of unusual subtlety.

Reconstructed in the 1930's by the Civilian Conservation Corps, La Purisima is the most comprehensive historical restoration in California. Original building methods were used – the work closely approximates that of the original Indian laborers.

CHRONOLOGY

1787 — December 8. Founded by Lasuén. Named "The Immaculate Conception of Mary the Most Pure."

1788 — First buildings begun.

1791 — Completed.

1812 — Destroyed by earthquake.

1815 — Moved to new site, new buildings erected.

1834 — Secularized.

1845 — Sold.

1874 — Returned to church, but sold because of dilapidated condition.

1935 — Acquired by State of California.

1937 — Restored.

Santa Cruz

Chapel, used for weddings and private masses, is not a replica, but contains relics and objets d'art. Pink windows give a warm glow to the interior.

Pleasant courtyard and fountain reflect mission spirit.

Emmett and School Streets, Santa Cruz

The little chapel that represents the old Mission Santa Cruz is an approximation, built at one-third the original scale.

Santa Cruz started with a good site, balmy climate, rich soil and friendly Indians — potents of a prosperous future. Building proceeded at a good pace. Within six years a quadrangle was completed, with workshops and a two-story granary. Millstones made in Carmel ground corn and wheat into fine flour.

Then trouble began. The governor founded a pueblo nearby and named it Branciforte to honor the viceroy. First settlers were a motley assortment: criminals, sick people and indigents, with one thing in common — undesirability. Latecomers of the same ilk joined them, engendering continuous friction with the padres and mission Indians. Partly because of the contamination of the bad pueblo, the mission never progressed. Maximum population was 523. It was among the first to be secularized. The cattle were sold, the remaining Indians faded away, and the land was granted to individuals.

CHRONOLOGY

1791 — August 28. Founded by Padre Lasuén. Named for Sacred Cross.

1793 — Building begun.

1795 — Construction, with quadrangle finished.

1834 — Secularized.

1840 — Bell tower collapsed.

1856 — Destroyed by earthquake.

1858 — Frame church built.

1889 — New church built.

1931 — Mission replica built, as memorial chapel, ⅓ size of original. Facade closely follows sketches of church built in 1795.

The little chapel is an approximation of the original at one-third size.

Nuestra Señora de la Soledad

Three Miles West of the Town of Soledad and Twenty-Five Miles South of Salinas in Monterey County.

Odd coincidence and friendly Costanoan Indians gave Soledad its name. Captain (later governor) Don Gaspar de Portolá and Padre Juan Crespi, with a band of soldiers, were marching north — up the Salinas Valley — in the hot summer of 1769, looking for the port of Monterey.

When they stopped to camp on the banks of a sluggish river, some Indians approached. Crespi tried to communicate with one of the men, but he couldn't understand him. However, there was a word that the man repeated that sounded like "soledad" — Spanish for loneliness. (Actually, in Costanoan, it probably meant "the people of this river.")

Two years later when Serra was returning to Carmel after founding San Antonio de Padua, he stopped at the same place, which had by now been selected as a mission site. He visited with the Indians and asked one woman her name. She replied with the same word — "soledad!" Serra thought deeply; and then and there decided on the name of the new mission. So the Indians chose the title for this mission Nuestra Senora de La Soledad — Our Lady of Solitude (one of the designations of the Virgin Mary).

The new community prospered at first. Padres directed Indians in tapping the Salinas river, providing ample irrigation. Broad fields supported herds of cattle, several thousand sheep and five hundred horses. Five years after its founding, the population was 727 and, in 1820, 2,000 conversions were recorded.

But in 1824, the Salinas River rose and destroyed the church. Again in 1828, floods washed away the chapel that replaced it. A smallpox epidemic killed Indians by the hundreds. The last minister, Sarría, died at the altar . . . Then the mission died, too. Indians looked elsewhere for better living. The Mexican government even took the *roof* to pay a debt!

Finally, in 1846, Soledad was sold by the governor. When restoration began a few years ago, the buildings had crumbled. It is now a mission of the parish of Soledad.

Where stone pillars were lacking, the padres simply produced them by having them painted right on the mission walls. Statue is "Our Lady of Solitude."

CHRONOLOGY

1791 — October 9. Founded by Lasuén. Thirteenth mission. Named for Our Lady of Solitude.	1831 — Collapsed.
	1834 — Secularized.
	1846 — Sold.
	1859 — Returned to church.
1797 — First church (thatch-roofed adobe) completed.	1963 — Padres' wing restored.
1805 — Enlarged.	1964 — Chapel restored.

In this view, one sees simplicity of design. Note Moorish-style door carving. Soledad was the link between Carmel and San Antonio de Padua.

Small but pleasant surviving portion of the mission is a tiny fraction of the original building complex.

San José

In Fremont, 15 Miles Northeast of San Jose.

Just before founding San José, Presidente Lasuén persuaded the viceroy to authorize five new missions and to send padres, supplies and implements. Lasuén was an early day salesman . . . he pointed out that he could save the viceroy $15,000 a year — the cost of military escorts — if the chain was filled in so there was no more than one day's journey between missions. Indians rarely attacked in daylight.

Lasuén set out with Sergeant Amador and a party of soldiers from Mission Santa Clara on Trinity Sunday, June, 1797. When they came to a hillock from which they could see both Mission Dolores and Yerba Buena Island, they planted a cross and named the mission: . . . San José de Guadalupe.

San José was a trouble spot from the start because of fugitivism. Many of its Indians came from the San Joaquin Valley — over the mountains and forty or fifty miles away. Alfred Robinson says the Indians "adored" their beloved missionary, Father Narciso Durán. But their love for the forest led them into fugitivism just the same.

Two outstanding missionaries, Buenaventura Fortuni and Narciso Durán ran San José for a long time. Durán was particularly versatile and talented. He later served two terms as missions Presidente. While he was at San José, he carved out a unique musical career. Though he had no formal training, he became an accomplished musician and teacher. He took Stone Age Indians who spoke nothing but Miwok, Mutsun or other dialects and had never heard any music except tom-toms, reed flutes, and rattles, and taught them to sing four-part harmony, Gregorian chants, masses and hymns. Then he developed a 30-piece band, devising practice instruments until real instruments arrived from Mexico.

Favorite mission motif – Moorish "river of life" pattern – is carved into the heavy planks.

Atypical decor lacks the rococo color and complexity of most mission interiors. Yet it has a simple beauty and dignity of its own.

CHRONOLOGY

1779 — June 11. Founded by Padre Lasuén. Fourteenth mission. Named for St. Joseph, patron of the Universal Church.

1797 — September — First church completed.

1809 — April 22 — New Building dedicated.

1834 — Secularized.

1846 — Sold.

1858 — Returned to church.

1868 — October 21 — Destroyed by earthquake.

1916 — and 1950 — Partly restored.

Among the largest of missions – the church is 190 feet long – sturdily built San Juan Bautista survived even though located right on San Andreas fault.

San Juan Bautista

Old bronze bell and front entry arch. Walls are four feet thick.

In San Juan Bautista, 4 Miles South of U.S. Highway 101, 17 Miles North of Salinas.

Finding oneself in the midst of a Spanish-California mission town in the 1820's has a pleasant "time-machine" effect.

This is San Juan Bautista, the only mission with three naves and the widest of all the mission churches in Califor-

nia. The mission forms the north side of the square around the old town plaza. Opposite are the Zanetta house and cottage, old wash house, plaza stable and the carriage and wheelwright shed. On the West, the Castro house and the Plaza Hotel. The East is bounded by old Camino Real, expanded from an Indian footpath and only 9 feet wide (you can still see the wagon ruts). Past El Camino are the rodeo grounds, and the fields of the San Benito River Valley.

A thriving trading center for hides, tallow and farm products, sprung up around the mission. Though it was a bit east of the original Camino Real, a loop was soon created to include San Juan, which formed a buffer between the Coast and the unruly Tulare Indians.

Still, problems with Indians occasionally culminated in raids. The mission was surrounded by a war party in 1798 . . . but the braves were persuaded to depart peaceably. Another time, Padre Arroyo de la Cuesta brought out a barrel organ and his music calmed the attackers so successfully that they not only declared peace for several years —

but a number stayed and joined the mission so they could hear the organ regularly!

San Juan Bautista grew rapidly with the help of friendly local Indians. A first crude structure was succeeded in seven months by an adobe church an in addition of a granary, barracks, monastery and some houses. When the padres were pondering whether or not to enlarge the structure, twenty days of earthquakes knocked down most of the walls, so they expanded while rebuilding. An elaborate new church — the present one — was completed and the governor with other notables attended the cornerstone-laying ceremony July 13, 1803.

Padre Cuesta was also a linguist and architect. It was he who designed the big church with three naves. Unfortunately, Indian participation dropped off at the time it was completed; the church was too big for the congregation and so the arches were filled in to gain solidity for earthquake protection.

The church is directly over the San Andreas earthquake fault but, due to relatively careful construction, important parts have survived. After the 1906 quake, it was rebuilt with steel, reinforced concrete and heavy cross-bracing so that it is considered safer now than ever before.

Inside the church, one can see wild animal prints in the floor. Newly formed tiles were set out in the field to dry. At night, deer, bobcats and other animals walked over them while they were still soft.

The interior was decorated, for board and room, by Thomas Doak, a temporarily stranded sailor from Boston. He and his Indian helpers, painting through 1818, used mostly gold and green; and with the red draperies behind the colored statues in niches, the effect is still bright, and definitely theatrical.

Front entrance has changed little since construction one hundred years ago.

CHRONOLOGY

1797 — June 24. Founded by Lasuén. Fifteenth mission. Named for John the Baptist.

1798 — First church completed.

1803 — Second, present church begun.

1812 — Dedicated.

1835 — Secularized.

1859 — Ground returned to church.

1906 — Damaged by earthquake.

1949 — Restored. Financed by Hearst Foundation.

The interior decorator, whose work remains as bright and alive as when he painted it in 1812, was Thomas Doak, a Boston sailor and first Anglo-American in the province.

San Miguel Arcángel

Original campanario still in use.

Ancient bronze bell is still in working order.

Unusual cactus garden embellishes courtyard.

On old Highway 101 in San Miguel, 9 Miles North of Paso Robles, Halfway Between Los Angeles and San Francisco.

In the busy summer of 1797, when three missions were founded by Padre Lasuén, he hurried to San Miguel to fill in the big gap between San Antonio and San Luis Obispo. The mission started with a bang . . . with a large crowd at the founding ceremony on July 25, when fifteen Indian children were baptized.

The first church, mud-roofed, was quickly built, served for a year, then replaced by a larger one.

The padres didn't tile the roof (biggest fire hazard), but even so the church lasted until 1806. By that time, real economic progress had been made . . . big herds had accumulated, a row of craft shops was active, and the granaries were full.

Then fire destroyed the buildings and 6,000 bushels of wheat, a huge quantity of wool, finished cloth and hides. It was a crippling loss. However, nearby missions helped by donating new clothing, implements and grain, and got San Miguel functioning again.

A new tile-roofed adobe church was completed in 1818. Its design is severe, but inside, one sees the striking decorations done in 1818 by Spanish artist Estevan Munras.

In the mission library, Munras found designs he liked and interpreted in rainbow colors that are still vibrant. He painted trompe d'oueil doorways and balconies on the walls and an elaborate reredos. Munras is commemorated in Monterey by a street, hotel (Casa Munras) and an old adobe building.

Like other missions, San Miguel attracted converts from the San Joaquin Valley. These Indians were called the Tulareños, named for the tule swamps beyond the mountains. The mission baptismal register reveals the names of numerous Indians from villages like Bubal, Telame, Yulumne, and elsewhere along the San Joaquin River.

Nonetheless, things went well for sixteen years — until secularization in 1834. Then San Miguel, along with all the others, was wrecked in the general collapse.

In 1846 notorious Governor Pio Pico disposed of the physical remains of the mission for $600 — all but the church and priests' quarters — to Petronillo Rios and William Reed.

The latter and his family, with some servants, used an entire wing for living quarters, despite the fact that the sale had been illegal and was disputed for years.

In 1848, Reed rode off to the Sierra gold mines, presently returning with sacks of gold dust. A bit later, he sold some herds of cattle and sheep for a good price.

San Miguel, at this time, was a stopping place for gold rush riffraff on their way from Los Angeles to San Francisco or vice versa.

Burro-powered grinding wheel once milled mission grain for the bakery which provided food for hundreds of Indians.

Fountain, not part of the original mission architecture, is a concrete copy of one at Santa Barbara.

Distinctive as the mission without a bell tower.

Spectacular reredos is one of the most striking in the mission system, a fantasy of color and design.

One day five deserters from a British man-of-war came by. Reed invited them to dinner. He let slip something about having hidden gold in the place. His words of braggadocio turned out to be his death warrant. The deserters departed, ostensibly to continue northward. But as soon as it was dark, they doubled back.

Attacking in force, the tramps murdered the unsuspecting Reed, his wife, children, servants and visitors — eleven in all. After literally tearing the building apart in a frantic, futile search for Reed's gold, they fled southward.

A hastily organized posse caught up with the murderers on the oceanside cliffs near Santa Barbara. In a bloody fight, one criminal was killed and another leaped into the sea and drowned. The other three were captured and taken to Santa Barbara, where they were promptly tried, convicted and hanged.

CHRONOLOGY

1797 — July 25. Founded by Padre-Presidente Lasuén. Sixteenth mission. Named for St. Michael, the Archangel.

1818 — Present church completed.

1821 — Decoration finished.

1834 — Last mission to be secularized.

1845 — Sold.

1859 — Returned to the church.

1901 — and 1928 — Main buildings renovated.

Fountain, red tile roof, corridor with arches – pleasing features of mission architecture, grace the courtyard.

San Fernando Rey de España

Colorful statue of King Ferdinand of Spain (1217 - 1252) is centerpiece of reredos.

1½ Miles West of San Fernando, Off U.S. 99 on San Fernando Mission Boulevard, Near Sepulveda Boulevard.

Four beautiful springs, looking as if they would never run dry, were the key to the location of San Fernando. In its heyday, 1819, the mission had 21,000 head of livestock and did a big business in hides, tallow, and leatherwork including shoes, sandals, saddles, door coverings, and rawhide strips for lashing structural members together.

When gold was found at Coloma in 1848, starting the great rush, it had already been preceded in 1842 by a mini-rush at San Fernando. A ranch foreman there was pulling up onions for his dinner, when he noticed bright gold flakes in the dirt. Soon a motley army of diggers arrived, but the bonanza was exhausted in a few months.

The mission went through the usual changes . . . secularization, decay, abandonment, restoration. There are architectural details of interest: some doors have peaked Mudejar arches, a blend of Moorish and Spanish style appropriate for the four-foot thick walls, with handcut "river-of-life" pattern doors and ornate wrought-iron locks.

Buttresses were installed after the 1812 earthquake, and proved successful in stabilizing structure.

Original olive press from San Diego mission is on display, as well as a mill stone for grinding wheat into flour.

CHRONOLOGY

1797 — September 8. Founded by Lasuén. Named for Ferdinand, King of Spain (1217 - 1252).	1834 — Secularized.
	1846 — Sold.
	1861 — Returned to church.
1799 — First church completed.	1879, 1912, 1916 — Restorations.
1806 — Present church completed.	1930's — Present restoration.
1812 — Damaged by earthquake.	1974 — Church Replaced.

San Luis Rey de Francia

Bright California colors, ancient arch, enliven courtyard of San Luis Rey, once one of the greatest of the missions.

Guadalupe Corner in Peyri's Court. Wall painting of the Mexican Madonna.

San Luis Rey, 5 Miles East of Oceanside, Off State Highway 76.

The central character in the history of Mission San Luis Rey de Francia is a charismatic padre — Antonio Peyri. He guided it from founding in 1798 until secularization (all the missions virtually disbanded by Mexican decree) thirty-four years later.

Besides unusual energy, good disposition, practicality and frugality Peyri had an innate talent for architecture. Building construction was a constant feature of life at San Luis Rey. His effort resulted in one of the best-designed and most beautiful of the churches.

In addition to the splendid edifice on a hill dominating the valley, there was an extensive layout for crafts and agricultural pursuits. Sunken gardens and a well-planned laundry complex in front, a spring system with a charcoal filter through which the water flowed to the fields, and six acres of buildings were arranged around a 500 x 500 foot quadrangle.

One incident illumines the warmth of Peyri's relationship with his Indian flock. When he foresaw the end of the missions, he requested and received permission to resign his post, and made secret plans to return to Spain. The Indians discovered his purpose and a large group mounted horses and galloped to the beach at San Diego just as his ship was pulling out of the harbor. They charged into the sea after him. Waist-high in the waves, they beseeched Padre Peyri to remain, but had to be content to receive his blessing from the deck as the ship sailed away. For years his Indian friends prayed for his return.

Sophisticated touch of Padre Antonio Peyri is apparent in this beautiful interior.

CHRONOLOGY

1798 — July 13. Founded by Lasuén. Eighteenth mission. Named for Louis IX, King of France, canonized in 1290 for Egypt and Holy Land crusades.

1811 — Present church begun.

1815 — Dedicated.

1833 — Secularized.

1846 — Sold.

1856 - 1892 — Abandoned.

1865 — Returned to church.

1893 — Rededicated.

Designed by Padre Antonio Peyri, this church is subtly different from other missions, with an effect that is sophisticated and professional.

Santa Inés

Companile is part of the front wall of the church.

Mellow afternoon sunshine at Santa Ines seems to reflect the golden past.

In Solvang, State Highway 150, 7 Miles East of Intersection with U.S. 101 at Buellton.

As at other fortunate missions, early success carried on to strong material prosperity at Santa Ines, which at its peak owned thirteen thousand animals and was famous throughout California for the excellence of Ines Indian craft products.

When Hippolyte Bouchard made his attack on the California coast in 1818, some of his men were captured by the Californios, among them Joseph Chapman and John Rose, the former an American, the latter a Scot. Chapman, employed at Mission Santa Ines in 1820, built a grist mill. In December of 1821 he received from Governor Pablo Vicente de Solá a document certifying that he was included in an amnesty granted by the King of Spain to all Anglo-American prisoners taken in the Bouchard invasion.

In 1822 Chapman went to Mission San Gabriel, where he built another mill. In the same year he was baptized a Catholic at Mission San Buenaventura by Father José Señán. Shortly thereafter he was married, at Mission Santa Ines, to María Guadalupe Ortega, whose father owned a large ranch in the vicinity.

Although he bought a house in Los Angeles, where he obtained land and planted a vineyard of 4,000 vines, Chapman continued to do odd jobs at various missions, where he was a great favorite with the friars. Apparently, he was unexcelled as a jack of all trades and could make or repair anything the missions might happen to need. And he edified the clergy as well. Father Sanchez declared it a marvel that one so long in the darkness of Baptist faith could give such example of true Catholic piety to older Christians.

After the Indian rebellion of 1824 Mission Santa Ines. like most other missions, experienced some measure of decline.

Ornate altar and reredos has gilt, green and red color scheme, typical of a number of missions.

CHRONOLOGY

1804 — September 17. Founded by Padre Estevan Tapis. Nineteenth mission. Named for St. Agnes.	educational institutions California — College of our Lady of Refuge of Sinners.
1817 — Present building dedicated.	1846 — Sold.
1836 — Secularized.	1862 — Returned to church.
1844 - 1846 — Temporary headquarters first	

Beautiful Santa Ines commands its lovely valley like a queen at a coronation.

Nothing tangible remains of San Rafael Arcangel. The reconstruction is an approximation created from scanty evidence.

San Rafael Arcángel

In San Rafael, 20 Miles North of San Francisco.

San Rafael was the only mission that began as a hospital, or *asistencia* for another mission.

Health problems at Mission Dolores were so tragic in the early 1800's, with Indians dying in hundreds, that something had to be done fast. For one thing, when they got sick, they needed somewhere warm and dry to get well. Trying to recuperate in the breezy, foggy climate of Dolores turned out to be a prelude to death for many. Changes from the natural life the Indians led before the arrival of their uninvited visitors weakened their constitutions.

Governor Sola recommended to Padre Ramon Abella of Mission Dolores, that convalescents be transferred to a place suggested by Lieutenant Gabriel Moraga of the San Francisco Presidio. The site, now San Rafael, has a sunny Southern exposure in the Marin hills, overlooking the Bay. Mt. Tamalpais sheltered it from chill sea winds.

A group of convalescents were bundled in blankets and rowed across the Bay, shivering in the fog. In a few weeks, Marin's salubrious climate accomplished wonders. The projected *asistencia* became reality. Padre Gil y Taboada volunteered to serve as director. He was appointed — an excellent choice since, of all the Franciscans, he was the most knowledgeable in medical matters.

As time went on, other Northern California missions sent patients to convalesce in the sun. The hospital grew, and was accorded full mission status in 1823, and by 1828 had a population of 1026.

For some time, San Rafael was the northernmost buffer against potential Russian expansion. It became a point of departure for groups of soldiers and padres scouting Northern California with a view to establishing missions at Suisun and Petaluma and a presidio at Bodega Bay. (The plan had the backing of government and church authorities but never materialized.)

Chapel was designed in contemporary fashion, but in harmony with mission motifs.

CHRONOLOGY

1817 — December 14. Founded by Padre Vicente de Sarria. Twentieth mission. Begun as a hospital asistencia for Dolores.

1818 — Church built.

1823 — Accorded full mission status.

Named for St. Raphael, patron of good health.

1834 — Secularized.

1841 — Sold.

1842 — Abandoned.

1855 — Returned to church.

Last of the missions to be built, Solano has been reconstructed to match style of the church in the 1840's.

San Francisco de Solano

Spain and First Street at the City Plaza, Sonoma.

The life of this mission was the briefest of all — nine years. It started and finished its life as a pawn in early California power politics.

Working at Mission Dolores, beset by bad weather, Indian epidemics and infertile soil, Altimira conceived the idea of abandoning Dolores and San Rafael and founding a new mission in Sonoma. Instead of going to his ecclesiastical superiors, he took his plan to Governor Don Luis Arguello. The idea was an instant hit. Expansion northward dovetailed with his own ideas. The Altimira-Arguello plan

was presented to the Territorial Legislature in 1823 and approved. The real authority lay in other hands. When Padre-Presidente Sarría discovered the scheme, he ordered work stopped. Three-way negotiations ended in a compromise. Altimira continued with construction of the Sonoma mission, without disturbing the *status quo* at Dolores or San Rafael.

Unfortunately, instead of using judgment and understanding, he relied on flogging and imprisonment to rule his small domain. Many Indians ran away to escape his temper. An angry band of those who remained stormed Solano in 1826, burning and looting buildings. Altimira fled for his life, luckily succeeding in reaching San Rafael, and returned to Spain. In 1834, Solano was secularized.

Old grape vines, red tile roof, four foot thick walls, convey typical mission atmosphere.

CHRONOLOGY

1823 — July 4. Founded by Jose Altimira. Twenty-first mission. Named for St. Francis Solano, missionary to Peruvian Indians.	1834 — Secularized.
	1838 — Razed.
	1840 — Present chapel built as Sonoma parish church.
	1881 — Sold.
1824 — Dedicated.	1903 — Bought by Historical Landmark League.
1827 — Replaced by larger church.	1913 — Restored.